THE **WRITER'S** GUIDE TO **POWERFUL PROSE**
dave bricker

THE **WRITER'S** GUIDE TO **POWERFUL PROSE**

By Dave Bricker
All Rights Reserved.
Copyright ©2015 Essential Absurdities Press

This book may not be reproduced, transmitted, or stored in whole or in part by any means, including graphic, electronic, or mechanical without the express written consent of the publisher except in the case of brief quotations embodied in critical articles and reviews.

Cover and book design by David Bricker.

ISBN: 978-0-9843009-9-0

ESSENTIAL ABSURDITIES PRESS

HONORARIA

To all who continue to inspire and encourage me on my writing path:

To Richard Geller who was the first of many authors to ask if I "knew how to design a book."

To the many remarkable writers for whom I've had the privilege of producing remarkable books.

To the marvelous friends who have read, commented, and edited my work over the years.

To Steven Bauer who showed me the value of working with a professional editor, even after all my talented friends contributed so much.

To Liz Cunningham for making me rewrite the introduction.

To the thousands of readers who visit and comment on my blog every week: You keep me writing.

To the readers of my books with whom I've had the honor of sharing my ideas, stories, and experiences.

To my family who understands.

For Eva

"We are all apprentices in a craft where no one ever becomes a master."

—Ernest Hemingway

"The difference between the almost right word and the right word is … the difference between the lightning bug and the lightning."

—Mark Twain

TABLE OF **CONTENTS**

Introduction 1
Bland Pronouns & Static Verbs 7
Think For Yourself but Dive With a Buddy 17
Come to Your Senses 21
Clichés 25
THAT Fat 33
Who's That? 35
Boring Words & Generic Descriptions 37
Shy Away From Timid Writing 41
Writing Dialogue: 49
Truth & Authenticity 55
How Long is Your Sentence? 63
Adverbs & *Bad* verbs 67
Stand Up. You Don't Need Those Crutches 71
Take Your And Off My But 73
Why Not Take All of Me? 79
Dots…! 81
Start an End to Beginnings 85
Now and Then 87
Television Land 91
Conclusion 95
About The Author 99
Colophon 101

INTRODUCTION

Whatever styles or genres you write in, if you want to become a better writer *quickly,* this book is for you. Novelists, business coaches, textbook authors, journalists, academics, and memoirists must all learn to battle the dark forces that oppose effective writing. Adapt the techniques you'll learn here to your tastes, purposes, and sensibilities to develop your personal writing style.

Whether you write literary fiction or technical manuals, powerful writing depends on the storyteller's fundamental elements of conflict and transformation. The conflict may be as simple as facing the challenge to master a new skill. The transformation may be as simple as proving your ability to successfully complete an exercise. Or the conflict may be abstract, metaphorical, or mythical. Dragons must be confronted and slain. Kingdoms must be saved. Evil must be defeated. Transformation can involve mundane tasks or life-changing personal, societal, or even planetary evolution.

The story of you becoming a powerful writer is the same. You, the protagonist, have set out on quest to master the alchemical art of turning thoughts, feelings, ideas, and opinions into tiny squiggles of ink on paper that inspire, educate, entertain, and ultimately transform your reader.

And this is not metaphorical magic; this is the *real stuff.* Consider Beethoven who was completely deaf. He composed symphonies *in his head* and converted them into lines and dots on paper. Over a century after the composer's death, musicians continue to read these ink spots, perform the music they represent, and mesmerize listeners.

But the only thing you'll find on the sheet music is *performance data;* a computer can read and execute it, but the performance will be uninspired. *Something else* happens when a human musician reads the notes. The performer taps into something mysterious and powerful that connects us all. Time ebbs and flows. Melodies crescendo and fade. Hints of vibrato, sustain, and subtle dynamics inject magic into the music—magic that can't possibly exist on the staff paper. To perform a musical piece is to connect with its creator across time and distance. And what was *it* that inspired the composer to write that music in the first place? What is the performer's—and the listener's—connection to *that* mystery?

The writer of prose likewise gets ideas from *somewhere,* and converts them into ink marks. As with music, a computer can translate them into understandable speech— we've all heard the soulless, robotic drone of text read by a microchip—but human readers convert this data through some inexplicable process back into powerful ideas, and experiences. Science cannot explain how something so ethereal as a thought or a feeling could be reconstituted from tiny marks on a page. But when we read, tears flow, laughter transports us, and new ideas redirect our thoughts and actions. Whether a book is a bible or a programming manual, it has potential, if written well, to connect us to *the mystery* and to bring about spiritual and intellectual transformation. *That's* storytelling.

Yes, there are magical, mysterious forces at work in the writer's art. The "powerful writer" alluded to in this book's title is one who has learned to connect both himself and his reader to *the mystery,* even if his subject matter is dry or practical.

What is the conflict that drives the story of you, the aspiring writer? What challenges must you overcome as you march toward your goal? In mythic storytelling parlance, the white wizardry of crafting powerful prose is plagued by goblins, gremlins, and demons that must be defeated before your transformation can be achieved.

Spelling goblins ruin the most eloquent of prose, though these are perhaps the easiest to spot with a bit of light countermagic. Digital spellcheckers ferret out most of them, though vigilance is required; your spellchecker won't sea the clever ones.

Every writer confronts *grammar* gremlins. Grammar gremlins cling to the undersides of your words, disturbing flow, obscuring meaning, and confusing readers. Experience is the strongest countermeasure. Write, study, and practice. As you grow, grammar demons will find it increasingly difficult to hide.

Most writers, even experienced ones, fail to see the *style* demons hiding in their writing. My purpose in offering this book is to teach you how to find and defeat them. These invisible saboteurs inhibit your power to communicate eloquently, boldly and directly. They prevent you from finding your own voice and style. They deter your reader from engaging with the pure meaning of your text. They impede the transmission of ideas, suppress your power to inspire, and weaken the connection between you, your reader, and *the mystery.* And because many style demons are grammatically correct, they are the most elusive of writing problems.

Friends, editors, other authors, and readers are analogous to the helpful elves, wizards, and spirits who impart wisdom as you journey toward becoming a powerful and effective writer. I am but one of many such guides you'll meet along your way. Though I have written and published several books of my own, and helped other authors publish many more, my background is in graphic design. This book draws as much on those experiences. Weak design is characterized by elements arranged haphazardly on the page; weak writing is no different. Writing and design (and musical composition) share a common goal: communication. The power of any of these media to achieve that goal relies on *design*—a process of *conscious* aesthetic decision-making informed by an awareness of patterns, structures, and techniques that facilitate (or hinder) the transmission of ideas and information.

Consider the graphic designer's awareness of kerning—the spacing of adjacent letters in text. I recall one design student's series of posters about child soldiers. His caption was supposed to read:

In War, There Are Two Types of Casualties

Unfortunately, because he paid no attention to kerning, his posters read:

In War, There Are Two Types of *Casual ties*

Becoming aware of something often requires nothing more than having it pointed out to you. The student, his colleagues in critique groups, and a thesis committee of MFA design professors all failed to spot the problem. And yet, here it is, as stark and bright as the full moon; it may as well be printed in blood.

The fashion styles of war notwithstanding, try an exercise I used to do with my own design students: Walk around an urban block and pay attention to kerning in public signage. You don't need to practice, meditate, conduct research, write scholarly papers, or attend classes to recognize poorly kerned type. Once you're aware of the horrific spacing problem, you'll see it everywhere;

the world is a poorly kerned place. Twenty minutes of walking and observing will change how you see and work with type forever.

As with graphic design, awkward prose is associated with certain style patterns. These patterns are easy to recognize and understand. Once you become aware of style demons and learn how to see them, your writing will improve *immediately.* You'll still spend time agonizing over word choice and sentence structure, but you'll be better at spotting potential problems and exposing them to a conscious aesthetic decision-making process.

Other writing problems discussed in this book, like the use of clichés, are not as easy to track down using your word processor's "find" function, but you can become aware of them, learn to see them, and cultivate an ability to use or avoid them consciously. The chapter on "Truth versus Authenticity" doesn't discuss writing style at all, but it addresses an important stumbling block for many authors.

This book was created to teach you today what you can practice for the rest of your life. We'll walk around the literary block, look at the signs, and learn to see style demons you didn't see before.

Read, learn, and grow. You'll be a better writer by the time you finish this book.

—Dave Bricker, Author

BLAND PRONOUNS & STATIC VERBS

Even experienced writers overuse pronouns. In our haste to move a plot forward or deliver a message, we lay out strings of facts involving nonspecific people engaged in nonspecific actions.

> We are sure it was him.

> We were there.

> He was standing nearby when we arrived.

Given sufficient context, these sentences define a sequence of events, but they represent a failure to transform a functional outline into an interesting narrative.

PRONOUNS

A pronoun is a "light" substitute for a noun. Pronouns are useful; there's nothing inherently wrong with them, but when not used carefully, pronouns become a crutch for lazy writers.

Pronouns at the beginning of a sentence run the risk of being vague, as by themselves, they don't mean much of anything—they refer to something *else,* something with substance. Never use a pronoun unless the noun to which it refers has already been used and the connection between the pronoun and that noun is made evident by their immediate proximity.

> It felt cold and heavy in his hand.

In context, the same initial pronoun can avoid repetition and smooth out the prose. In the following example, the reader has no doubt about what "it" is.

> Tom withdrew the revolver from his coat pocket. It felt cold and heavy in his hand.

Look for an opportunity to substitute a detail or a synonym or a pinch of pepper for the pronoun. Can you insert a phrase that builds tension or supports a thread of the plot?

> Tom withdrew the revolver from his coat pocket. His father's gun felt cold and heavy in his hand.

Use of the simple pronoun "it" is not wrong, and electing to use it is a valid writing choice. But when designing your prose, search out each instance of "we," "they," "he," "she," "there," and "it." Make a *conscious decision* about whether you want to use a pronoun or substitute some spice.

STATIC VERBS

Pronouns have an unfortunate affinity for "static" verbs; they're often found clinging to each other.

> We were on top of the mountain.

> He was a sailor with a sparkling blue uniform.

> They are delicious.

These verbs are all forms of "to be," and they're the literary equivalent of equal signs in math. Verbs of *doing* are much more interesting than verbs of *being*. Verbs like "was," "are," and "is" represent the most generic possible statements a writer can make about the status of a subject. If verbs like these were single, they'd advertise that they "like candle-lit dinners and walks on the beach." They perform a functional role in a sentence by fulfilling the requirement that it contain a verb, but that's all they do apart from asserting existence and tense.

"There are" and "There is" are particularly troublesome combinations.

there: in some nonspecific place, state, or condition

is / are: exists in some nonspecific way

Another example:

There were two flavors of ice cream in the freezer.

For an easy fix, put the subject up front.

Two flavors of ice cream were available in the freezer.

Or put the subject in back (to force better verb choice):

The freezer contained two flavors of ice cream.

Try playful, active verbs to characterize the freezer:

The freezer offered two flavors of ice cream.

The freezer concealed two flavors of ice cream.

Upgrade the verbs in the following sentences. Add an action, some conviction, some sensory input. Make the sentences more experiential.

We were on top of the mountain.
We planted our flag on top of the mountain.

He was a sailor with a sparkling blue uniform.

He stood proudly at the rail, a sailor with a sparkling uniform.

They are delicious.

They taste delicious.

Now replace the pronouns. Identify who or what is being represented and add details that enhance description or experience.

Our trio of exhausted climbers planted our flag on top of the mountain.

Midshipman Thomas stood proudly at the rail, a sailor with a sparkling uniform.

Sarah's homemade chocolates taste delicious.

Remember our grad student with his "casual ties?"

In War, There Are Two Types of Casualties

Assuming he fixed his kerning, a stronger slogan would have been:

War Brings Two Types of Casualties

Or perhaps not; the "best" way is up to you. You may prefer to let the original, bland "there are" add contrast that helps the reader focus on "War" and "Casualties."

Strong writing does not require every instance of a pronoun combined with a generic verb to be "fixed." A pronoun and generic verb combination fulfills the simple role of converting a potent phrase into a sentence. Sometimes, less is more. Deleting all pronouns and static verbs is not our goal; *recognizing and questioning them* is our objective.

It was a dark and stormy night.

In Edward Bulwer-Lytton's classic example, the only reason the pronoun and generic verb exist is because "dark and stormy night" wouldn't be a proper sentence without them. Nevertheless, I would be tempted to open with, "A dark and stormy night." and let the stalwart grammarians hang.

Part of the "design process" is having the taste to know when it's *inadvisable* to translate the "is" construction into something "better." Stark, simple, concise writing has its place. Elmore Leonard said, "If it sounds like writing, I rewrite it." Instead of automatically "fixing" every sentence that begins with a pronoun, fix enough of them to avoid "hypnotic repetition."

Consider the following example. Can you find the pronoun-verb combinations? (You can write in this book; I promise not to tell.)

Johnson was a stern man with a square jaw and a bristly moustache. He walked with a limp, and he was known to stir his coffee with his finger. He was an honest and principled man, despite his rough demeanor, and he was well liked by the students of Bunsen Township.

There was one thing he couldn't abide: a sentence starting with a pronoun and a static verb. He approached the lecture hall with a magazine folded haphazardly under his arm.

We went quietly into the classroom, knowing that today, we would witness the rhetorical crucifixion of yet another editor. We had five minutes before the starting bell, but we went quickly to our seats, put our books on our desks, and waited.

In the highlighted version below, not all the verbs are static and not all the nouns are pronouns, but the repetitive sentence structure clogs up the flow of the prose.

Johnson was a stern man with a square jaw and a bristly moustache. He walked with a limp, and he was known to stir his coffee with his finger. He was an honest and principled man, despite his rough demeanor, and he was well liked by the students of Bunsen Township.

There was one thing he couldn't abide: a sentence starting with a pronoun and a static verb. He approached the lecture hall with a magazine folded haphazardly under his arm.

We went quietly into the classroom, knowing that today, we would witness the rhetorical crucifixion of yet another editor. We had five minutes before the starting bell, but we went quickly to our seats, put our books on our desks, and waited.

Much is arguably *right* about the example. The narrative paints a portrait of a colorful main character. Mounting tension drives the simple plot. We understand that Johnson commands the respect of his students. But the prose is gobbered up with repetitive sentence structure and weak verbs. Try reading the highlighted text out loud; the pattern will jump out at you. Once you see and understand the problem, you'll be able to exert conscious control over how you use or avoid this common writing pattern.

Here's one possible rewrite:

> Sam Johnson limped across the quadrangle, pausing to stir his coffee with his finger. He gazed sternly, his bristly moustache perched over his square jaw. But despite his rough demeanor, the students of Bunsen Township liked the professor and respected him as an honest man who stuck to his principles.
>
> Johnson couldn't abide one thing: a sentence starting with a pronoun and a static verb. He approached the lecture hall with a magazine folded haphazardly under his arm.
>
> We filed quietly into the lecture hall, ready to witness the rhetorical crucifixion of yet another editor. Five minutes remained before the starting bell, but we quietly took our seats, placed our books gently on our desks, and waited.

Your edited version will be different from mine; you might choose to leave some of the text as is.

BLAND PRONOUNS & STATIC VERBS

I debated changing:

> There was one thing he couldn't abide: a sentence starting with a pronoun and a static verb.

because I like the "stark rhythm," but chose to honor the spirit of the exercise. Every instance of a pronoun with a static verb becomes a cue for you to consider whether the prose should be improved.

Common writing patterns sound more or less the same from one writer to another. Creative substitutions reveal your individual, personal writing style.

Use your word processor's "find" function to track down common pronouns and "generic" verbs in your manuscript. If the process of inspecting every "it" or looking at every sentence in your manuscript that begins with "There" is laborious, you've probably overused these pronouns and will find the effort worthwhile. For each instance, evaluate whether the language used is simple and elegant, or a wasted opportunity to write something better.

25 POPULAR PRONOUNS

it	me	everything
I	him	someone
you	one	themselves
he	her	everyone
they	us	itself
we	something	anyone
she	nothing	myself
who	anything	
them	himself	

THINK FOR YOURSELF BUT DIVE WITH A BUDDY

This book offers advice about writing patterns, but such patterns are proposed as cues for making assessments, not as writing rules. You might *deliberately choose* to employ some of the writing patterns I avoid. My editor, Steven Bauer, challenged my previous chapter with the following example:

> "In the fall the war was always there, but we did not go to it any more. It was cold in the fall in Milan and the dark came very early. Then the electric lights came on and it was pleasant along the streets looking in the windows. There was much game hanging outside the shops, and the snow powdered in the fur of the foxes and the wind blew their tails. The deer hung stiff and heavy and empty, and small birds blew in the wind and the wind turned their feathers. It was a cold fall and the wind came down from the mountains."

The "hypnotic rhythm" of the highlighted phrases, and the repeated words like "fall" and "blew" and "wind" make this passage "clunky" *to me*. The paragraph starts off by mentioning the war and then turns abruptly and incongruously to describe the streets of Milan in the fall. Static verbs abound. The repetitive sentence structure makes the paragraph sound like a list of factoids; the rhythm of the repeated phrasing pattern becomes hypnotic.

Trying to salvage the colorful and relevant elements, I revised it:

> "Milan was cold in the fall. Dark came early. How pleasant it was to look into the windows along the streets when the electric lights came on. Much game hung outside the shops. The deer hung stiff and heavy and empty. Snow powdered in the fur of the foxes. The icy wind blew their tails and turned the feathers of small birds as it whistled down from the mountains."

Steven Bauer responded:

This opening paragraph of Ernest Hemingway's "In Another Country" is identifiable as his from a mile away; it has all the trademarks of the Hemingway style—short declarative sentences connected by conjunctions; a bare minimum of subordination; diction pared down to its bones (no fancy language, no Latin derivatives); and sharp stunning detail. The narrative voice here is flat, uninflected, as one might expect from a deeply depressed member of the walking wounded (the "war" is World War I), but we don't learn the circumstances of the narrator until later in the story. Hemingway used style partly as a form of characterization, and his effect on 20th century American prose was astonish-

ing. Maybe you're objecting to the effect he's had on American prose. Readers are either stunned into admiration by the effects he manages with his choices (as I am) or they think it's dull writing that could be improved (as you do). This is more than anything, I think, about aesthetic approaches.

One style does not fit all. A choice that a writer might make in one place would be a bad choice in another; each instance is distinct and each subject can be approached in myriad ways. It's all a matter of syntax, diction, tone, rhythm, all adding up to a complex almost indefinable effect.

There is no one style that is better than another, and any time an editor suggests a revision, he or she had better be channeling the author rather than some abstract notion of "good writing."

—*Steven Bauer, Editor*

Though Steven Bauer's taste deviates from my own here, his comments reinforce the principle behind this book—that powerful writing comes not from doing it *this* way, but from doing it *your* way. Write any way you think "works," but do so consciously, intentionally, and consistently after having studied your options.

One more lesson that may seem out of place in a book about self-editing techniques: Authors rarely expose the exchanges they have with their editors as I have above, but *even professional editors hire professional editors.* I may presume to have sufficient expertise to write a book about writing, but I wouldn't make that presumption public without pressure-testing it. This book will help you engage in deeper and more productive conversations with an editor, but it's no license to swim alone. Polish your prose and develop your style with the techniques suggested here. Then work on the fine points with an experienced professional. A 100,000-word book with 1000 errors in it is still 99% correct; the odds of producing a technically perfect book—even *with* a good editor—are slim. You write for the purpose of communicating with others. Why would you *not* engage a critical reader to ensure you're accomplishing your communication goals?

Some writers are afraid an editor will rewrite their work and remove their authentic, personal voice from the writing. Editing is not "sending your work out to be processed." It's a highly collaborative process where critique and discussion help you express yourself effectively in your *own* style. If even one of the writing concerns addressed in this book improves your writing awareness, you'll have tasted the benefits of working with an editor—and of me working with mine.

COME TO YOUR SENSES

Writing teachers encourage us to engage the mind and senses. Describe sights, smells, tastes, sounds, feelings, thoughts, and tactile experiences to appeal to the reader's imagination on every possible level.

In concept, this is excellent advice. In practice, the advice often gets taken too literally. Think of "saw," "heard," "felt," "tasted," "smelled," and "thought" as a special category of the boring verbs discussed in the previous chapter. Use them, but use them consciously and sparingly.

> After so many days of hot, endless sand, José saw green mountains rising above the horizon.

> Ben awoke in a bright room, unable to recall how he got there. "I must be dead," he thought as he listened to distant choral music.

> Maria stared at the pile of crumpled one-dollar bills and felt ripped off.

> George smelled barbecue and rushed over to the grill.

These sentences describe characters and what they're experiencing, but they're weak because the *narrator* is relating the sensory descriptions. Remember another piece of classic writing advice: *let your characters tell the story.* Build direct relationships between your characters and your reader by keeping the narrator's voice from getting between them.

This advice can be expanded. Let the *settings and objects* in your scenes tell the story. Inanimate objects and places can rise, wave, beckon, impose, threaten, welcome, suggest, produce, radiate, and even speak. As always, balance is key. The transference of human thoughts and feelings onto inanimate objects should honor certain intuitive boundaries. Mountains might "call to" or "look down on" José or "rise" before him, but they shouldn't "jump for joy" or "ask for his email address."

> So many days of hot, endless sand. At last, green mountains *rose* above the horizon.

Presumably, we already know José has been walking in the desert. The reader will assume that whatever you describe is what José sees.

> Ben awoke in a bright room, unable to recall how he got there. *I must be dead.* Choral music filtered in from some distant place.

Focus on describing the stimuli rather than on describing what Ben *thinks* about them. The italics reveal his reaction without having to tell the reader, "Here's how he reacted."

> Maria stared at the uninspiring pile of crumpled one-dollar bills. *What a rip-off!*

Again, the italics provide the character's unspoken inner voice, but by adding an adjective ("uninspiring") to describe the bills, the reader understands what *provoked* the reaction.

> The sweet, tangy, smoky scent of barbecue wafted through the open door. George rushed to the grill.

George's reaction is a no-brainer. By emphasizing the stimulus (the scent) instead of the response, the reader will beat George to the hibachi.

Describe the perceived rather than the fact that it *was* perceived to draw readers directly into your characters' experiences.

CLICHÉS

The following example is a bit long because of the nature of the exercise. Read it all if it makes you smile. Or read a few paragraphs and then skip to the discussion if you get the point and prefer to move on.

> Since time immemorial, clichés have sneaked in the door when we least expect them to. They're low-hanging fruit for writers who abscond with them quickly instead of striving for excellence. But to the trained eye, writing clichés stick out like a sore thumb. Authors of this day and age who struggle under the yoke of undetected style errors are too numerous to mention. The capable writer puts his nose to the grindstone and embarks on a quest to find hidden treasure. With the patience of Job, he leaves no stone unturned in his search for words and phrases that give his writing a personal, authentic voice.
>
> Writers from all walks of life are determined to publish by hook or by crook. Champing at the bit to publish his book, the writer gets behind the eight ball and pours himself lock, stock, and barrel into the task of writing. Cool as a cucumber and lost in contemplation, the ambitious author taps away at the keyboard day in and day out until the crack of dawn, happy as a kid in a candy store. As his manuscript grows by leaps and bounds, he

envisions a whirlwind bookstore tour and expects his book to sell like hotcakes. Sure of success, he pulls out all the stops and pours everything but the kitchen sink into his writing. And he's proud to have sufficient skill as a writer to avoid paying through the nose for an expensive editor. Publishing, he is certain, will open the floodgates to a world of opportunity where there's never a dull moment. He envisions untold wealth, living larger than life in the lap of luxury, and laughing all the way to the bank.

But this flurry of activity is actually the calm before the storm. The pie-in-the-sky dream is too good to be true. Such writers are accidents waiting to happen. In this dog-eat-dog world, such books are usually dead in the water, and at best they're a flash in the pan. Give the devil his due; the writing is on the wall for this author. His own worst enemy, he fails to realize that his chances are one in a million. Little the wiser, he jumps the gun and publishes before you can say "Jack Robinson." At the end of the day, how many of his words fall on deaf ears? He falls hook, line, and sinker for the fantasy of becoming a bestselling author. Then, to add insult to injury, he hangs on to the bitter end, enjoying at best only a checkered career before his book is buried beneath the sands of time and forgotten by the long march of history. For all intents and purposes, in the twinkling of an eye, he's dead as a doornail.

It goes without saying that the winds of change have brought higher standards to the fast-maturing world of self-publishing. Self-publishers are all in the same boat. To tame the wild horse of the publishing world, we must all pay the piper and nip bad writing habits in the bud.

CLICHÉS

Clichés are only one problem among many that writers should avoid like the plague. Each and every one of us must take the tiger by his tail and think outside the box. New words and phrases are easy to find or create for those willing to take the journey. The challenge to find clever words is hardly a search for a needle in a haystack. Why use clichés over and over when there are plenty of fish in the sea? Why live the writer's life on borrowed time? After all, you can't make a silk purse out of a sow's ear. Make no bones about it; writers who count their chickens before they're hatched will soon find them coming home to roost. The ball's in your court. Take the bull by the horns, bite the bullet, go back to the drawing board, and add some clever new phrases to your bag of writing tricks. Open up that can of worms in your writing before you publish and share them. The acid test for good writing is authenticity. Well-constructed prose is a breath of fresh air, not a rehash of the same old same old. Learn the ropes. Dot your Is and cross your Ts. Knuckle down and honor the craft of writing.

All things considered, it's probably a fool's errand to try to rid your writing of clichés entirely, but in a nutshell, it stands to reason that in the cold light of day, weak writing habits will all come out in the wash. Publishing without paying your dues is like banging your head against a brick wall. Instead of shooting yourself in the foot, take the high road. The path to excellence is as plain as the nose on your face. Play your cards right, face the music, strike while the iron is hot, and turn over a new leaf.

You'll find no hard and fast rules about what's clichéd and what's not, but by the same token, writers who exercise discerning judgment about their wordcraft are head and shoulders above the rest. Practice makes perfect. Put your best foot forward and work slowly but surely until your writing becomes as steady as a rock. For all intents and purposes, your prose need not meet the lofty standards of the average ivory tower stick in the mud, but when it comes down to the nitty-gritty, polished writing is a rare beast indeed and not anything to be sneezed at.

Without a shadow of a doubt, too many authors make the same mistakes *ad infinitum*. Gluttons for punishment, they dismiss previous, failed efforts as water under the bridge and part of the learning curve, then forge ahead. Come hell or high water, they're determined to earn the glowing tributes, thunderous applause, and choruses of approval that only a chosen few are blessed to receive once in a blue moon.

But there's no such thing as a free lunch. Publishing is a game of survival of the fittest. Ignorance is bliss. Mark my words, the time has come to stop muddying the waters of short, sweet, and to the point writing with the cast-off jetsam and flotsam of language. The unvarnished truth: writers who fail to heed this warning will get their just desserts. Proof of the pudding is that left high and dry, and subject to twenty-twenty hindsight, they cry "sour grapes" at the moment of truth, and tuck their tails between their legs. With ruffled feathers, they throw in the towel and meet the untimely end of their literary lives.

As luck would have it, capable writers are not expected to be able to quote the thesaurus chapter and verse. Becoming a powerful writer does not involve reinventing the wheel. As a matter of fact, there's no need to make a mountain out of a molehill; becoming cliché-aware requires no painstaking investigation. There's no need to search your writing high and low—and ultimately, whether a phrase is "officially" a cliché or not is anybody's guess. Cultivating an ability to recognize clichés is nothing to write home about. Not to put too fine a point on it, writers who seek out and expose themselves to one of the many online lists of clichés will, after due consideration, naturally incorporate their newfound awareness into their writing.

First and foremost, those writers who ultimately hit the nail on the head are the ones who recognize that battling style errors is part of the long haul every one of us must make. The completion of a rough draft is a mixed blessing. The savvy author must put his money where his mouth is, stick to the straight and narrow, pay his dues, and turn his diamond in the rough into a polished gem. Writers worth their salt know that the first draft is only the tip of the iceberg.

Great writing requires tender loving care and when the work is done, the polished author may yet wind up an unsung hero. Excellent writing won't necessarily make or break a book and regrettably, some authors grow sick and tired enough to give up, get some well-earned rest, and publish, warts and all. But make no mistake; you get what you pay for. Your excellent book may not make you rich but you can bet your bottom dollar it will be a sight for sore eyes in a world where quality and attention to detail are sorely needed. If you don't care, who will?

Last but not least, just for the record, this essay is hardly short and sweet but there's a tongue-in-cheek method to my madness. As strange as it may seem, I sincerely hope that readers who take my words with a grain of salt will see them as a blessing in disguise.

If I were to highlight the clichés in the above essay, I'd be left with little unhighlighted material. We speak and write clichés every day because they are convenient and well-understood carrying handles for commonly communicated ideas.

Clichés offer marvelous insights into the evolution of language; every cliché has an associated story. The writer who understands the roots of the clichés in his arsenal thinks of each one as a story encapsulated in a phrase. In studied hands, these clichés become powerful tools.

As the writer of several nautically themed books, I encountered clichés rooted in maritime traditions. In the days of wooden ships, heavy anchors were raised from the bottom by a group of crewmembers who would wind them around a windlass—a large cylinder with protruding winding handles. The phrase "weigh anchor" is still used today, despite the fact that a mechanical windlass spares the crew the "weight" of the anchor on their shoulders.

Was a "windlass" originally a device that prevented sailors from getting "winded," or a device that prevented sailors from having to "wind" up the anchor by hand? The roots of the term are quite literal; "windlass" is derived from 13th century Anglo-French and Scandinavian sources meaning, "a device for raising weights by winding a rope round a cylinder." The colorful roots are imaginary.

Such misinterpretations and shifts in meaning are not uncommon. A vessel "under way" is commonly thought to be "making her way" through the water. The term evolved from "under weigh," which indicated the point at which the anchor in the process of being raised had parted from the bottom and the (engineless) ship was officially in motion.

"Hanging on to the bitter end" is another cliché with a seafaring origin. One end of a rope was fastened to the ship; the other end was fastened to the bitts (cleats or bollards) on the dock. "The bitter end" makes a useful metaphor for someone suffering failure and defeat, but it came from practical, literal, mechanical circumstances. The "bitterness" of "the end" was never an intended association.

Now that you know the backstories behind these clichés, will you ever use them the same way again?

Many clichés are burnt out; let them rest. "Thinking outside the box" just isn't "outside the box" anymore. A "sight for sore eyes" isn't worth looking at. Your "bottom dollar" isn't worth betting if you have a wallet full of credit cards.

Some clichés degrade into meaningless gibberish over time. It isn't a "doggy dog world" out there; it's a "dog eat dog world." When it's time to "toe the line," don't "tow" it, even if you have a "tow line" on your boat.

Visualize the metaphors that made clichés powerful before they became clichés. When your character "flies off the handle," imagine the damage caused by an axe blade doing the same thing. Picture the destruction caused by a "loose cannon" on a rolling ship's deck.

Do you know when you're writing clichés or do you absentmindedly blurt them out? The key to growth is self-awareness. Find a list of clichés on the Internet and challenge yourself to write an essay that uses as many of them as possible (as in my exercise at the beginning of this chapter). In doing so, you'll make a conscious connection with each of them. Later, you'll be surprised (but aware) when you catch yourself using them.

Instead of banning clichés from your vocabulary, put them in a special drawer in your literary toolbox. Use them intentionally, instead of automatically, to expose more of your writing process to the influence of conscious aesthetic decision-making.

THAT FAT

"That" is often useless fat that slows down an otherwise elegant sentence. Fortunately, misuse of "that" is one of the easiest writing patterns to find and evaluate.

> I think that you and I need to talk.
> I told my readers that I would post an article about writing.

Two scoops is particularly fattening:

> I think that that is a capital idea.

The use of "that" as a conjunction for *introducing a subordinate clause expressing a statement or hypothesis* is technically correct, but in many cases, "that" is superfluous; it adds no clarity. The example sentences function just as well without it.

> I think you and I need to talk.
> I told my readers I would post an article about writing.
> I think that is a capital idea.

Of course, "that" can help to differentiate between "this" and an array of other choices. In my "two scoops" example, I underlined the second "that" because that one isn't the "that" that's causing the problem. "That" is fine when used as a pronoun or an adjective.

> Could you hand that to me? (used as a pronoun)
> I don't like that sentence. (used as an adjective)
> That's what it takes to be a writer. (used as a pronoun)

Our own style habits are often invisible to us, but words like "that" can be easily searched for and found with your word processor's "find" function. Locate each occurrence of "that" in your manuscript and make a conscious decision about whether to leave or delete it.

Sometimes, you'll find that an unnecessary "that" sounds better. Leave it.

Sometimes "that" is used correctly as a pronoun or adjective. Leave it.

Like great design, great writing is a process of subtraction. Use "red flag" words and writing patterns to get the objective handle you need to track down and eliminate fat from your writing.

And that is that.

WHO'S THAT?

A common mistake is to confuse "who" and "that." While you're searching for unnecessary examples of the "fat" explained in the preceding chapter, watch out for another common misuse of the word "that."

> She's the girl that loves me.
> My boss is the only one that cares about the late project.
> I'm looking for the man that hit my car.

When talking about people, use "who."

> She's the girl who loves me.
> My boss is the only one who cares about the late project.
> I'm looking for the man who hit my car.

In my house, animals are people. I use "who" to refer to them, too.

> *Who* spread pillow stuffing all over the floor?

Use "that" for inanimate objects.

Where's the bag that holds my stuff?
Here's the toy that I tripped over.
Here's the sentence that ends this short chapter.

BORING WORDS & GENERIC DESCRIPTIONS

Generic descriptions are telltale signs of lazy writing. Add color to your writing by replacing overused and boring words.

> It's such a nice day today.
> He's very bright.
> My dog is really cute.
> Bill is a good soccer player.
> Shari is in a bad mood today.
> I received some happy news in my mailbox.
> Barbara was sad to see Jim leave.

These words are commonly used in speech; they're close-at-hand when we need a description on the fly. But unless a writer is intentionally emulating informal speech, these words make watery, vacuous, and weak additions to written prose.

Use your word processor's "Find" function or a tool like AutoCrit.com to sniff out generic descriptions and boring words. You'll find a few false positives among the clunkers:

THE WRITER'S GUIDE TO POWERFUL PROSE

In 1989 I sailed to Great Abaco Island.

but you'll also find great opportunities to substitute more impactful language.

Give every description conscious attention. Don't depend on the words and patterns we naturally gravitate toward when we speak; most of us use the same jokes, adjectives, adverbs, and pat phrases over and over. Avoid letting "easy talk" find its way into your writing. The best writers go back, isolate the descriptions, and ask themselves, "Does this add the required tone, color, and intensity?"

John had a good time at the party.

Boring.

John had a splendid time at the party.

A bit old fashioned.

John had a magnificent time at the party.

This last example uses flowery words for their own sake. Overwriting is as big a problem as underwriting. Balance is key.

Sometimes, the presence of a generic description is a cue that your narrative needs—well—more narrative:

John successfully limited himself to two drinks. He spoke to a cute young woman with dark hair and intelligent-looking glasses for over an hour without saying anything stupid or regrettable, ate at least $30 worth of shrimp, and managed to snap a photo of Harold's painting without being observed—and all on Hanman's dime.

The above example transcends the simple description of John's experience. John accomplishes something and moves the plot forward. Each internal description reveals something about John's tastes, values, behavior patterns, and motivations—as if we readers were there at the party observing him and forming our own conclusions. Few words are dedicated to anything other than painting a picture of John "having a good time at the party"—so we don't have to explicitly state that to the reader. While writing a draft, generic descriptions serve as placeholder text, like a fluid outline. Get the thought on paper, move on, but come back later to add spices and garnish.

Descriptive words have "intensity" analogous to color saturation. Words like "good" and "bad" are black and white; they're functional and clear (and granted, sometimes the ideal word choice) but they lack potency or nuance. Other words like "splendiferous" and "gargantuan" can perhaps be likened to hot pink or international orange. Words like "awesome" and "ominous" may once have been colorful but their intensity has faded from overuse.

As with visual arts, well-crafted prose comes from careful and mature assessments of hue, saturation, texture, and tone. Learn to recognize generic descriptions. Use them as cues for questioning your word choices. Examine a word and its synonyms to explore different shades of meaning and color.

BORING WORDS

A Lot	Hear	Seriously
Awesome	Hot	Slow
Bad	Interesting	Short
Beautiful	Kind	Small
Big	Fast	Soft
Cold	Like	Sweet
Dirty	Literally	Tall
Dry	Little	Totally
Easy	Loud	Ugly
Good	New	Nice
Fun	Old	Cool
Happy	Really	Very
Hard	Sad	So

SHY AWAY FROM TIMID WRITING

Several styles of writing can appropriately be described as "passive," but because that term already has a defined meaning, this chapter refers to them as "timid."

To clarify, "passive writing" refers to a specific set of grammatical circumstances where emphasis switches from subject to object.

The money was stolen by Jill.

instead of

Jill stole the money.

This is confusing if you're writing about Jill but perfectly acceptable if you're answering a question about what she stole.

Timid writing is the bad habit of humble authors. Especially when writers first start out, they don't want to appear arrogant or overly assertive so they avoid absolutes in favor of merely admitting possibility.

> It might rain.
> It could get better.
> This may be the answer.

Timid writing is characterized by wishy-washy woulda-coulda-shoulda language. Usually, it's not grammatically incorrect; it's just weak. Bold writing is not arrogant; it's confident and direct—things you *should* be as a writer. Try these suggestions:

> It's going to rain.
> Things will get better.
> This is the answer.

Of course, you may actually wish to speculate or express uncertainty. "Would," "could," "might," and "may" are useful, valuable words but when mishandled, they're unnecessary; they dilute the strength of a sentence. The weather forecaster doesn't want to lose credibility with viewers by saying it "might rain." To avoid timid style, he qualifies his "maybe" with calculated odds—even if they're reliably unreliable.

There is no ultimate arbiter of good or bad or right or wrong. Treat specific words and writing patterns as "flags" for the application of conscious, objective, aesthetic decision-making.

Here are some more examples of timid writing:

> Every day, I would hear the *tap tap tap* of his mallet against his chisels; this would have been some time in 1967.

> John could see the sun rise every morning.

In the above cases, the "timid" voice detracts from the impact of the sentence. These are not events that *would have* or *could have* happened; they're events that *did* happen. Here are suggested fixes:

> Every day, I heard the *tap tap tap* of his mallet against his chisels; this was some time in 1967.

> John watched the sun rise every morning.

None of the suggested corrections changes the author's voice or tone—this is how professional editors work—but the statements are now more direct and easier to understand.

As with other writing patterns, you won't want to change every occurrence of timid writing; sometimes that voice is appropriate. Sometimes, the "music" of the writing sounds better that way; leave it alone. The point is to make a conscious decision.

Timid usages are often characterized by the use of "helping verbs" like "was" and "were" paired with participles (words that end in "—ing.") A search for words that end in "—ing" will turn up opportunities to choose objectively between "was/were —ing" and "—ed."

> Bill was looking at the painting.
> The geese were flying south.

Though the static verbs "was" and "were" are valid indicators of past tense, they're not necessarily timid. Search for them in your manuscript; your personal writing style will be revealed. If you find too many static verbs and too many timid forms, the laborious task of upgrading your sentences will train you to be a better wordsmith.

Generally, if something happened in the past, use the past tense unless you're writing about a past situation when someone was not sure what was going to happen in the future. Look for "was" and "were" and then look for "would", "could", "might", and "may."

> Bill looked at the painting.
> The geese flew south.

"Has" and "had" and "have" add a timid tone to a sentence when misused. You'll have to skip past a lot of correct usages but you'll also get a chance to examine each sentence through the lens of, "Does it speak directly, or does it fail to look the reader in the eye?"

SHY AWAY FROM TIMID WRITING

The past perfect tense is the correct tense to use when referring to an action that occurred before another action—a "toggle switch" that alerts a reader to a flashback or flashforward in narrative writing. For example:

> John was a pudgy, chain-smoking stockbroker, but in high school he had been captain of the wrestling team.
>
> Ed has always played bluegrass music but tonight he is going to play jazz.

The examples below feel "timid" because the author doesn't state what happened with authority. The events are past tense and complete, but the sentences awkwardly mix past and past perfect tenses. Ask yourself when the events happened and apply the appropriate tenses. If there's a switch from past to present or a switch from a general state to a specific one, use past perfect to make the change clear.

> My suspicion is that a rift had developed between them; Joe had left the family fold at a young age.
>
> I had gained business experience, honed my performance skills, and had developed my stage persona.

Because these sentences tell of no switch in state, they work better in past tense.

> I suspect a rift developed between them; Joe left the family fold at a young age.

> I gained business experience, honed my performance skills, and developed my stage persona.

Or you could mix things up in the first example, with one event coming before the next.

> I suspect a rift had developed between them; Joe left the family fold at a young age.

Other common flag words for timid writing are "about" and "just."

> Ben was about six feet tall.
> I'll be there in about ten minutes.
> I just want to eat.

Readers will forgive you if Ben turns out to be an inch shy of six feet or if you arrive in nine minutes and forty-six seconds. If you're hungry, say so directly.

> Ben was six feet tall.
> I'll be there in ten minutes.
> I want to eat.

"Seems" is also timid and overused. Unless you're intentionally sharing a feeling or suspicion, or are in the process of forming a solid conclusion that you're not yet ready to commit to, "seems" is the epitome of timid writing. "Seems" should rarely be used, except when you consciously intend to declare you're unsure.

> Correct: It seems like I've heard this advice before.
> Correct: The rain seems to be letting up.
> Correct: Jeff seems to be a trustworthy confidant.
> Timid: The play seemed to go on forever.
> Timid: Mary underwent a seemingly magic transformation.

Don't condescend to readers by cueing them to the fact that you're using a metaphor. They know the audience didn't grow old and die during the play. They understand that nobody cast a spell on Mary.

> The play went on forever.
> Mary underwent a magic transformation.

Timid writing is shy, indirect, insecure, vague, and tentative—things you *don't* want your writing to be unless you intentionally choose that voice for a character expressing uncertainty.

Learn to recognize the patterns that characterize timid writing and use them to control the strength of your prose. If you're going to write timidly, do so by design and not by habit.

WRITING DIALOGUE: HE SAID. SHE SAID.

Dialogue presents challenges for writers. Some prefer to simply declare what was "said." Many authors feel that "said" is both traditional and invisible. Some writers emphasize the speaker before what was said (as in the first line below). "Said" becomes less visible at the beginning than at the end of a sentence because the spotlight gets aimed at the speaker:

> Bill said, "I'm going to write some dialogue."
> "I look forward to reading it," said Helene.

But this style is *not* invisible. A narrator is telling us what happened—as if the characters spoke in some other time and place and we're hearing a play-by-play of their conversation *after the fact*. "Said," is *past* tense. Some readers object to the mindless repetition of "said," "said," "said."

This latter objection is all-too-often countered by inserting an exhaustive list of synonyms that fill in for the functional-but-dry "said":

"Let's try some sample dialog," suggested Bill.

"I'll give it a shot," muttered Helene.

"What shall we talk about?" asked Bill.

"Doesn't matter; this is just an example," responded Helene.

"You really should take this seriously," Bill admonished.

"Well, think of a topic, then," Helene snorted. "How can we have a serious chat about nothing?"

As the writer runs out of words, the narrative begins to take on unusual and unexpected colors that distract the reader from what's being *said*. And if the exchange is long, even writers with huge vocabularies *will* run out of synonyms and be forced to start recycling. The dialogue takes on quirky, bland, or journalistic overtones.

Some writers avoid dialogue, placing the burden on the narrator to relate the story directly to the reader:

> Once more. Say you are in the country; in some high land of lakes. Take almost any path you please, and ten to one it carries you down in a dale, and leaves you there by a pool in the stream. There is magic in it. Let the most absent-minded of men be plunged in his deepest reveries—stand that man on his legs, set his feet a-going, and he will infallibly lead you to water, if water there be in all that region. Should you ever be athirst in the great American desert, try this experiment, if your caravan happen to be supplied with a metaphysical professor. Yes, as every one knows, meditation and water are wedded for ever.
>
> —Herman Melville, *Moby-Dick*

WRITING DIALOGUE: HE SAID. SHE SAID

When characters are talking, ensure that the reader always knows who is speaking. At the same time, keep the narrator "off-camera" as much as possible so the reader feels *in the room,* listening to and watching the conversation.

I refer to the "narrator" because I encourage writers to take useful cues from film directors. Actors (characters) are the central focus on-stage, but the cameraman, the lighting crew, the soundman, and the director all have important jobs to do, *including staying out of the shot.* If Bill is speaking to Helene, the camera might look at Helene over Bill's shoulder, but in writing, where there is no camera, someone must *narrate* the facial expressions and gestures that reveal the characters' thoughts and feelings. If a "camera" exists in the mind's eye of the reader, the narrator serves as a director who makes unobtrusive signals to the "cameraman."

What's *unspoken* is often the most powerful part of the conversation. Powerful writers share important details without distracting readers from the dialogue.

> Bill took a long, deep breath. "I'm here to help. Rather than get upset, let's rewind, pick a topic, and move forward together."
>
> Helene looked down. "You're right. I'm sorry I jumped on you."
>
> "Water under the bridge, Helene. I'm over it." He put his hand on her shoulder, lightly. "Tell me what you're interested in—or what you ate for breakfast. I'm sure we can find a topic."

> Helene's eyes brightened. "You know that little restaurant on the corner of 5th and Main? The one with the funny blue awnings where they always forget to turn the 'we're closed' sign around?"
>
> Bill smiled at Helene's observations. He liked the way she picked out unusual details that anyone else would miss.
>
> "They make this French toast with rum in the batter you wouldn't believe. The bread has nuts in it and they have real maple syrup and …"
>
> Bill noticed the syrup stain on the ruffles of Helene's white blouse and suppressed a chuckle. *Nuts and rum; that explains everything.*

This dialogue is cinematographic. The narrator doesn't need to tell us which character is speaking; we're capable of assessing that on our own; that's what the quotation marks are for. The narrator's job is to fill in details that won't come through in pure dialogue: pauses, breathing, eye and hand motions, body language, facial expressions, clothing. It's not enough to *hear* the dialogue. If we can *visualize* it, we're *there* with the speakers. The narrator is still with us—much like a stagehand who is there with a bright spotlight—but we focus on where the light is pointed rather than on its source. The italics at the end offer Bill's unspoken thoughts. He doesn't want to offend Helene by stating his conclusions out loud, but we're privy to them all the same.

WRITING DIALOGUE: HE SAID. SHE SAID

In general, if somebody thinks or says something, let that character think or say it directly. Let the narrator's voice paint a picture of anything else the reader needs to understand and visualize the scene.

In the following dialogue from John Steinbeck's *The Grapes of Wrath,* the material outside the quotation marks is just as powerful as the verbal exchange, a perfect balance between the narrators and the "actors."

The owner drummed his knee with his fingers. "Deputy sheriff comes on by in the night. Might make it tough for ya. Got a law against sleepin' out in this State. Got a law about vagrants."

"If I pay you a half a dollar I ain't a vagrant, huh?"

"That's right."

Tom's eyes glowed angrily. "Deputy sheriff ain't your brother-'n-law by any chance?"

The owner leaned forward. "No, he ain't. An' the time ain't come yet when us local folks got to take no talk from you goddamn bums, neither."

"It don't trouble you none to take our four bits. An' when'd we get to be bums? We ain't asked ya for nothin'. All of us bums, huh? Well, we ain't askin' no nickels from you for the chance to lay down an' rest."

The men on the porch were rigid, motionless, quiet. Expression was gone from their faces; and their eyes, in the shadows under their hats, moved secretly up to the face of the proprietor.

Pa growled, "Come off it, Tom."

Engaging dialogue contains more than an exchange of words. Effective prose transports the reader into the scene—something that's nearly impossible unless you describe the scene and what the characters are experiencing. Having a character *say* what he's thinking is easy. Having him *show* you what he's thinking, sometimes without saying a word, is a hallmark of strong writing.

TRUTH & AUTHENTICITY

This chapter discusses a *thought pattern* rather than sentence structure issues, but it warrants inclusion in this book because so many writers get stuck in the quicksand that lies between truth and authenticity.

I attended a nonfiction-writing workshop where I was told that to qualify as nonfiction, a work must adhere to truth as strictly as possible. But such an edict rests on the naïve assumption that truth itself is knowable. The clean, white dividing line between fiction and nonfiction is, itself, a fiction. Truth is as nebulous as fantasy.

The contrived rule about writing only the truth is responsible for thousands of books that would have been excellent were they not burdened with unnecessary details. Thousands of others never get written because the would-be author can't figure out how to transform a long chain of linear facts into an engaging story.

In the late 1980s and early '90s, I spent a number of years living aboard a small sailboat, traveling through the Bahamas, crossing the Atlantic to Gibraltar, and living among a community of inspiring, colorful people who chose life afloat over terrestrial existence. I made several attempts to write my stories, and finally published my memoir twenty years later.

I began by writing individual stories, one at a time. Eventually, I collected almost fifty. I placed them in mostly chronological order and began to work them into a book with a single story arc that tied them together. Fifty short stories became one long one.

For research, I dug into my past and conducted interviews with people who were "there," some of whom I hadn't spoken with for two decades. Opening long-closed doors was scary and exhilarating, and it revealed curious things about the nature of truth. As I asked questions, reminisced, and listened to the stories of those who shared pieces of my adventure, I found they remembered things I didn't. I remembered things they couldn't recall. Some of the things we both remembered, we remembered differently: "No, that was me who said that to you!" If some absolute, factual version of truth lies beneath the memories, perceptions, and other aspects of consciousness that filter reality, getting at it is a fantasy. Facts are colored by memory, viewing angle, and time. Truth is an unattainable absolute.

After my father had cataract surgery, he remarked, "I never realized how yellow my world had become until I got these new lenses!" Was he seeing a less-than-accurate version of the truth before his operation? Or can we assume everyone sees things a bit differently—all of us looking through our own personal filters that prevent us from seeing that "ultimate reality?"

Our love of truth is natural and instinctive. We love movies "based on true life events," exposés, unauthorized biographies, inside stories, investigative reports, secret shoppers, and even gossip that *might* be true. We read because we're driven to find out who stole the diamonds, to understand how to invest and win, to know the secrets of the pyramids, and to reveal the mysterious workings of politicians, programming languages, and pocket watches. Even fiction writing is judged, at least in part, by its plausibility—by the strength of its foundation in truth.

For writers, truth comes in at least two flavors: essential and literal. The literal truth is the domain of scientists, journalists, and academics. The essential truth is the purview of effective storytellers. Your book on real estate investing is probably quite literal, but by changing the names of the people in your case studies and omitting the addresses of the properties they bought and sold, you deliver the essential truth—the *essence* of your message—while protecting people's privacy. Such alterations to the literal truth are hardly dishonest; they prevent extraneous details from obscuring your intended meanings and messages.

I was advised once (jokingly) "never to let the truth stand in the way of a good story." Certainly, such a practice could be used to mislead people—a "good story" should never be built on a foundation of lies, distortions, or omissions of critical facts—but given a certain purity of literary intent, *authenticity* is of greater value than literal truth. I wrote my memoir to commemorate special people, places, and times. Occasionally, I made up minor characters or snippets of dialogue because these helped the narrative flow (as if details of 20-year-old conversations can be remembered accurately, anyway). I always made sure these fabrications were plausible; any of them could have happened; they were fictional but *authentic*.

I worked with two writers whose love story included an exchange of emails that documented their growing openness and attraction to each other. They felt reluctant to alter the originals, but I explained, "Back when you wrote those emails, you weren't worried about making literature. Now that you're sharing these letters with readers, they have different jobs to do; they have to move a story forward—a story you didn't even realize you were writing; they need to constantly clarify to the reader who is speaking to whom, a non-issue when the two of you sent and received them; and a small sampling of them have to reveal progressive insights into what each of you was feeling as the relationship developed. Life does not unfold in eloquent prose. Instead of documenting exactly what was written, why not create email conversations that authentically represent your two voices?"

The resulting revision was much easier to follow and read, and it did a more effective job at honoring the authenticity of the exchange—even if it was less factually accurate.

Some memoirists have baggage to dump, some are narcissists, and some need a place to put their mid-life angst—but the best of them create my favorite reading material. Antoine de Saint-Exupéry's *Wind, Sand, and Stars*—his stories of flying mail across the mountains—are breathtaking. Memoir is not written so the writer can talk about himself for 400 pages; memoir is written to share experiences, insights, and perspectives. It may be *about* the writer but it's *for* the reader.

As such, the difference between documenting and storytelling is important. Documenting is about presenting facts; storytelling is about creating meaning. You're probably not short-changing your reader if you share what happened before your sixth birthday in a few short paragraphs—or skip those events altogether. You may elect to cut out important life experiences because as powerful as they were to you, they're tangents that don't move your core story forward. And if you visited two islands on one trip and three more on another, rolling their descriptions into a single, imagined voyage will spare your reader quite a bit of unnecessary sailing time.

Though we all want future generations to read about our lives, this is not why most memoirists create their books. Why *do* memoirists tell their stories?

The "official" history was written by "official" historians. If you were there and know what really happened, why not set the record straight and honor those who changed the world without recognition?

Our great-great grandparents lived in a time before cars, electricity, antibiotics, and anesthesia. Stories of their lives set against colorful descriptions of their times make for fascinating reading today. They encountered loss, love, war, sickness, and the trials of life as much as anyone does today, but they didn't have the powerful and convenient vehicles for researching and preserving history that we do; many of their stories died with them. If you are fortunate (or unfortunate) to have a powerful story, why not document and share, especially if you have experience, meaning, and wisdom to impart to others?

Memoir writing is the "extreme sport" for authors.

I want to take you there and then. If you sail with me, I want you to taste the salt. When the seas are up, I want you to feel queasy. If I can connect you to a unique place and time to experience colorful people and remarkable events, and, as a narrator, not ruin that experience with my presence, I'll have accomplished a tricky piece of storytelling. Authenticity is the ultimate writing challenge.

> Hove to, *Journeyman* rides comfortably among enormous swells, but contrary to first impressions, the wind has increased. From horizon to horizon, the surface of the ocean is a field of

churning white foam. The tops of giant rollers are blasted into flying spray by the wind. I am adrift at the center of an exploding world.

Why am I not afraid?

—from *The Blue Monk,* by Dave Bricker

HOW LONG IS YOUR SENTENCE?

Varying the lengths of sentences and paragraphs is an easy way to make your prose more interesting.

Many authors are afraid to write short, simple sentences. Academics, especially, reach for long words and complex sentences, thinking they'll impress their professors and colleagues with windy, run-on, pseudointellectual hyperbola. Confusing *complicated* with *eloquent* is a fatal mistake. Overwriting is boring, pretentious, and weak unless you're a practiced master of the Victorian style.

> Mr. Micawber roused me from this reflection, which was blended with a certain remorseful apprehension of seeing Steerforth himself, by bestowing many encomiums on the absent Littimer as a most respectable fellow, and a thoroughly admirable servant. Mr. Micawber, I may remark, had taken his full share of the general bow, and had received it with infinite condescension.
>
> —Charles Dickens, from *David Copperfield*

What about the other extreme? Search for "one-sentence paragraph" on the Internet and you'll mostly find questions asking whether writing them is even an acceptable practice. The one-sentence paragraph is not only "legal," it's a useful and powerful literary device.

One-sentence paragraphs are common when short pieces of dialogue are being exchanged, but consider the effect of serial one-sentence paragraphs in other contexts. The following excerpt describes my ocean crossing in a small wooden boat:

> The sun marches over our heads through a field of blue, burns the horizon beyond our wake, yields to the stars, purples the east, and rises before us again.
>
> We are aground in a river of time.
>
> We eat.
>
> We sleep.
>
> With the wheel, we turn the ocean round our boat.
>
> Days pass like silken threads on hidden currents of wind.
>
> Hours hover like dust revealed by a sunbeam.
>
> Forever collapses into a moment.
>
> There can be no other side, no destination.
>
> There is only here, only now.
>
> The wind falls light again.
>
> We motor over calm, shimmering seas.

The narrative reflects on the passage of time at sea. Though it could have been written as a single paragraph, consider how isolating each thought affects the pacing.

HOW LONG IS YOUR SENTENCE?

This is a marriage of prose and poetry, intended to be "read aloud" in your head. Pause at each comma. Stop at the end of each sentence. Let the words ring.

Consistent single-sentence paragraphs are not a requirement; this is writing, not math. In the following example, short sentences balance long ones.

> The sun falls below the pines of Great Abaco.
>
> The wind picks up.
>
> The temperature drops.
>
> We drag my dinghy to the top of the beach and prop it on its oars behind us to serve as a windbreak. John had the foresight to gather dry firewood back at Man-O-War Cay. We add to his collection a few pieces of driftwood we find on the beach. Behind our dinghy shelter, a small flame begins to consume our branches and wood scraps.
>
> Yellow sparks crackle and fly high into the fast-darkening night.
>
> Stars gather overhead.
>
> John points into the brilliant sky. "See the three planets grouped in a small triangle there? They're what we've come here for. They won't appear this close together again for over a thousand years."

Have you ever taken a photograph of a sunset? The resulting image inevitably fails to capture the glory of the scene; a sunset cannot be put in a frame. Sometimes, effective writing requires the author to create a detailed portrait, but "paint by numbers" also works. Your reader has seen sunsets before, experienced cold, and sat near a fire. Offer clues to help your reader construct his own picture from his own memories.

Short, single-line paragraphs mimic the experiencing mind. Experience, in its pure form, transcends words. More words might convey the author's picture of an experience at the expense of the reader's. Why place your reader in your head when you can pull her into your scene?

They say, "The devil is in the details."

So get rid of extraneous details.

Write succinctly and seriously. One-sentence paragraphs cue your reader to stop and reflect.

Victorian verbosity is as valid a writing style as postmodern minimalism. A book full of one-sentence paragraphs would be as ineffective as a book full of long-winded exposition. Read your work aloud. Does it let you pause to breathe or does it ramble endlessly? Are important thoughts set apart or lost in a thicket of overwritten prose? Does time pass at the pace you intended? You don't need to count words; develop a sense for "short, long, and medium" sentences. Mix and balance to achieve the desired effect.

ADVERBS & *BAD*VERBS

Adverbs add flavor to verbs, but many of them (especially those ending in —ly) qualify as their own category of cliché. Adverbs used without careful consideration often turn into *bad*verbs.

In particular, —ly adverbs are far too obvious a choice to use at the beginning of a sentence.

> Initially, I thought the adverb added a conversational tone.
> Basically, this is a weak sentence.
> Actually, this one is even weaker.
> Fundamentally, the —ly adverb adds nothing to this example.
> Suddenly, I can write better prose.

Initial adverb sentence structure is not technically wrong, but it's one style among many possibilities. Use it sparingly and on purpose.

You'll find boring adverbs involved in some of the other patterns we've discussed. Some—like "very," "really," and "truly"—are high on the list of commonly used generic descriptions.

> I'm <mark>very</mark> pleased to find out about adverb abuse.
> Understanding this will <mark>really</mark> help my writing.
> This knowledge is <mark>truly</mark> a gift.

Learning to recognize boring adverbs will help you quickly de-fluff your writing. Readers will safely assume that pleased is *pleased* enough, that the help you received was genuine even if you didn't declare it be *real,* and that you're expressing yourself *truthfully.*

> I'm pleased to find out about adverb abuse.
> Understanding this will help my writing.
> This knowledge is a gift.

Some adverbs infer that the writer lacks confidence in the prose.

> <mark>Suddenly</mark>, a genie appeared.
> This was <mark>seriously</mark> unexpected.
> Babu <mark>obviously</mark> knew what to do next.
> He <mark>absolutely</mark> had to ask if he'd be granted three wishes.

If you have to tell your reader something happened *suddenly,* perhaps it's because you didn't describe the scene adequately? If the event was unexpected, how could your character even know about it, never mind be *serious* about it? If his next move is obvious, shouldn't it be *obvious* to your reader? Under such extreme circumstances, is it necessary to clarify that the character's convictions are *absolute?*

> Babu rubbed the lamp gently against the sleeve of his robe. A powerful explosion hurled him to the floor and filled the cavern with blue smoke.
>
> Wide-eyed and trembling, Babu observed a powerful figure silhouetted against the swirling vapors. The tall, muscular man placed his right hand on his chest, extended his left hand, and bowed low.
>
> *A genie! I wonder if the rest of the legend is true.*

The rewritten passage focuses on *storytelling*. Given Babu's extraordinary circumstances, it's a waste of words to tell the reader the event was *sudden, unexpected,* or demanding his *absolute* attention; he was "hurled to the floor" by an explosion that left him "wide-eyed and trembling." The events and Babu's responses to them are more powerful and revealing than a boring adverb.

Much as the narrator should avoid interfering with dialogue, he should avoid interfering with the *story*. If he needs to step in and tell us an event was *surprising* or *serious* or *obvious,* it's time to write another draft.

A discussion of adverbs would be incomplete without mention of the most abused word in the English language—*literally*. "Literally" means it happened *exactly as it's being told*. I'm reminded of a radio interview I heard featuring a famous movie actor. When he said, "the script literally blew my mind," I imagined his head flying apart with chunks of exploded gray matter flying through the air. *Literally* does not mean *figuratively*.

> **Correct:** As the world-record holder, he's literally the fastest swimmer in the world.

> **Incorrect:** This chapter literally makes me want to kill someone.

The second example is (hopefully) a gross exaggeration of the literal truth, a *figurative* statement.

Use your word processor's "find" function to find instances of "ly " (include the space after the y) and "ly." Consider whether your adverbs are pulling their weight or adding fluff.

STAND UP. YOU DON'T NEED THOSE CRUTCHES

"Crutch words" are empty filler inserted into speech when we can't think of what to say. Obvious examples are "like," "well," and "you know."

> This whole thing is like, you know, some sort of bad dream. It's like, well, imagine if your whole world just like crumbled around you. Have you ever, like, felt that, you know, that well, you just can't get a break?

I heard two sports announcers on the radio who both inserted "you know" so often that I was unable to hear anything else they were talking about.

> "Blah blah blah you know blah blah you know?"
> "Well, you know blah blah, blah blah blah blah, you know."

Spoken crutches are contagious like *measles*. Avoid them and people infected by them or you'll soon sound like them.

Spoken crutches don't usually find their way into written prose, but written forms are common.

> In a manner of speaking, crutch phrases are a virus infects your prose. Suddenly, you may find yourself adding extra words to your sentences. At the end of the day, your writing will be better without them. Going forward, you should try to eliminate them. In all fairness, you may be using crutch phrases without realizing it. Needless to say, paying closer attention to your word choice is the only solution. Ultimately, you'll have to do something to overcome bad writing habits. So, what's your plan?

Crutch words and phrases share the stage with *bad-*verbs, generic descriptions, and clichés; you'll find plenty of overlap. Crutch phrases show up when writers want to appear friendly and conversational instead of stuffy and academic. When writing about dry topics (like writing patterns), the temptation to "lighten things up" is powerful.

Crutch phrases are so common, they're invisible—fluff that dilutes the effectiveness of your writing. Insert humor, warmth, levity, and humanity into your writing by being authentic, funny, clever, and warm—not by packing the cheeks of your sentences with literary cotton balls

TAKE YOUR *AND* OFF MY *BUT*

Sometimes we're thinking one thing, *and* then we want to add another thought, *and* then we want to add another. Associations trigger additions; such is the way the mind works.

This works well enough for spoken language, *but* the written word rests on a foundation of planning and editing. Sometimes, sentences flow more smoothly without conjunctions like "and." And, though some scholars disagree, you might wish to begin a sentence with "And" or "But."

If only for the sake of variety, consider the value of using a semicolon to distinguish two separate but connected thoughts.

> I'm hungry, and I want to eat.

> I'm hungry; I want to eat.

Both of the above examples are correct, but consider what happens when the phrases get long.

> This is a clear violation of State and Federal law, and I believe I'm well within my rights to contact the authorities.

One solution is to divide the long sentence into two shorter ones.

> This is a clear violation of State and Federal law. I believe I'm well within my rights to contact the authorities.

But dividing one sentence into two obscures the connection between the two thoughts. The second statement is a conclusion based on the first. Here, a semicolon offers the "stopping power" of the period while maintaining the dependency between the second phrase and the first.

> This is a clear violation of State and Federal law; I believe I'm well within my rights to contact the authorities.

The conjunction "and" lends itself to run-on sentences. Search for the word "and" with your word processor's "find" tool. Evaluate whether each instance should be left as-is, or if a semicolon or period better suits your style and intentions.

"But" is another commonly abused conjunction.

> Seattle is beautiful, but Miami is sunnier.

The sentence is short so we can leave it alone. When the example gets long and ponderous, we have the same choices as before.

> I saved for years to buy a beautiful instrument, but now that I have it in my hands, I can't find the music I was hoping to discover.

Break the sentence in two:

> I saved for years to buy a beautiful instrument. Now that I have it in my hands, I can't find the music I was hoping to discover.

Or use a semicolon.

> I saved for years to buy a beautiful instrument; now that I have it in my hands, I can't find the music I was hoping to discover.

The conjunctions "and" and "but" specify whether the two thoughts complement or contradict each other, but if the statements are well written, the relationship between them won't require explanation.

This gives you three "flavors" for compound sentences. Choose among them consciously. Don't rely on whatever style you were taught in high school.

A few notes on semicolons:

The two phrases should be able to stand on their own as grammatically correct sentences. Join them together to create a relationship between them, but don't join a sentence to a phrase.

Incorrect: It makes me ravenous; smelling that food on the grill.

Semicolons are also used as "supercommas" to separate lists of lists:

The teams wore red, white, and blue; green, yellow, and red; and blue and white uniforms.

Another common style error is to use "And" or "But" at the beginning of a sentence when you *should* be using it as a conjunction. Use initial "And" or "But" when you wish to interject an additional, independent thought.

Strong: I've been excited about this concert, and I'm ready for it to start.

Weak: I've been excited about this concert. And I'm ready for it to start.

Strong: I bought my ticket the day they went on sale, but my seat was in the balcony.

Weak: I bought my ticket the day they went on sale. But my seat was in the balcony.

Strong: I resolved to quietly take my assigned seat. But guess what happened next?

Weak: I resolved to quietly take my assigned seat, but guess what happened next?

Strong: An usher came up to me with an apology and a backstage pass. And I got to hang out with the band after the show!

Weak: An usher came up to me with an apology and a backstage pass, and I got to hang out with the band after the show!

The difference has to do with whether you want to connect two thoughts of relatively equal importance, or if you want to "interrupt" your first thought with another of *greater* importance.

Balance variety against consistency. Knowing your punctuation options will open up a surprising array of expressive opportunities.

WHY NOT TAKE ALL OF ME?

Totality, in its many forms, is often one more species of fluff. Do these adverbs need quantifying?

> Edgar felt totally confused.
> Carmen was completely exhausted.
> I slept through the whole movie.
> Juan couldn't eat his entire sandwich.
> My friends all came to the party.
> I'm all finished with my manuscript.

Edgar was either confused or he wasn't. It's not as if his degree of confusion or Carmen's level of exhaustion offers any insight into a story—and who has ever been *partially* exhausted? Unless I got bored and slept through the *end* of the movie, readers will assume I slept through all of it.

> Edgar felt confused.
> Carmen was exhausted.
> I slept through the movie.
> Juan couldn't finish his sandwich.

> My friends came to the party.
>
> I'm finished with my manuscript.

Unless you wish to clarify that only *some* of your friends showed up, and unless the ratio of attendees to no-shows is valuable to your story, expressions of totality are often unnecessary. Does it matter if a few of your friends got better offers and blew off your shindig? Use "some" or "part of" when that distinction is necessary. Otherwise readers will assume you mean "all."

A complementary style problem worth mentioning is unnecessary diminution.

> I have a bit of a headache.
>
> I'm spending a little time with my sweetheart.

Such usages are hardly egregious, but considering whether they're needed is hardly a waste of time.

> I have a headache.
>
> I'm spending time with my sweetheart.

As with other style demons, your word processor's "find" function will quickly locate instances of "all," "totally," "completely," "whole", "entire", "little", and "bit" in your manuscript. Consider whether sentences containing these words are better off without them.

DOTS...!

EXCLAMATION MARKS

Two commonly overused punctuation styles are exclamation marks and ellipses.

Exclamation marks provide a way to give emphasis, volume, and intensity to a sentence. Don't use too many.

> Ziggy gripped his paintball rifle. *Today I'm going to taste combat!* He nodded his head at Jack who had sought shelter behind a fiberglass boulder. "Cover me! I'm going to pop up, run right through the middle, and spray those guys!"
> Jack grinned. "Go for it! I'll keep them pinned down!"

Emphasizing *every* sentence is like emphasizing *none* of them; every added exclamation mark dilutes the effectiveness of the previous ones.

Exclamation marks should be applied to thoughts that are genuinely remarkable. Advertisers append exclamation marks to every imaginable form of trivia, but authentic writing does not rely on "artificial sweeteners."

We're having a big sale on corn chips!

My flight will arrive five minutes early!

ELLIPSES

The ellipsis is commonly mistyped with three periods. For convenience, many word processors will substitute an ellipsis for you if you type three consecutive periods, but the ellipsis is its own single character (option/alt-semicolon on your computer keyboard).

Use an ellipsis instead of a preceding or trailing emdash to indicate a continued, unfinished, or interrupted statement that trails off into silence (*aposiopesis* for the obscure vocabulary word collectors in the audience) where no particular dramatic emphasis is required.

Think of the ellipsis as a word. Put spaces around it (or not) as you would any other word. The ellipsis should have a space inserted before and after it to separate it from the text, but when combined with other punctuation, the leading space disappears and the other punctuation follows. Commas, question marks and other punctuation come immediately after the ellipses.

The following thought trails off. No spaces are needed, and no period follows as the sentence is unfinished.

"I studied all last night but I don't remember the answer. I just can't find..."

The following ellipsis is used to omit material from a quotation. It's a placeholder for missing words so treat it as a word and type a space before and after it.

> We, the people, in order to form a more perfect union ... do ordain and establish this Constitution of the United States of America.

An ellipsis at the end of a sentence with no sentence following should be followed by a period (for a total of four dots).

> Once upon a time there was a princess.... And they lived happily ever after.

The ellipsis is used in mathematics to mean "and so on." In a list, between commas, or following a comma, a normal ellipsis is used.

> 1,2,3,...100

The ellipsis is frequently abused in casual email exchanges where it indicates the writer is thinking, doesn't care to finish a sentence that has an obvious meaning, or that the conversation will be continued later. Filling your writing with ellipses is the literary equivalent of stuttering, muttering, and stammering. Use this technique for short passages only when you want to stutter, mutter, and stammer—with the understanding that too many ellipses will make your writing much more difficult to read.

> Let me check my calendar … okay, I'm free tonight.
> See you later …

START AN END TO BEGINNINGS

Many write absently about "starts" and "beginnings."

> John started to talk about his feelings for Vera.
> Ed began the long trek to the computer repair shop.
> Jill began to grow a set of fuzzy, brown mushrooms on her head.
> Jeanne started to feel as if nobody else cared about the garden.

But unless the narrative concerns the specific point in time or space from which an event commences, *starts* and *beginnings* are so much filler. Don't write about leaving the dock if your story is about the voyage.

> John talked about his feelings for Vera.
> Ed made the long trek to the computer repair shop.
> Jill grew a set of fuzzy, brown mushrooms on her head.
> Jeanne felt as if nobody else cared about the garden.

Save references to starts and beginnings for abrupt changes, turning points, and new actions. Use "started" or "began" to indicate a starting point from which developments expand or contract.

After years in prison, Mario began a new life.

Marco grabbed the top sheet of paper off the tall stack, sighed, and started reading.

Danny paused at the top of the slide and then started down.

The villagers began to collect in the park, arriving one-at-a-time at first, and then in increasingly larger groups, until the last of them had squeezed in to hear Brenda speak.

NOW & THEN

When you write about "now," does that mean "now" in the reader's context, or "now" when your book was published? Will "now" still be "now" when your book is thirty years old?

> People once wrote with pencils and paper; now we use typewriters.

In storytelling, "now" indicates a change of state from old to new.

> The genie granted Babu his first wish. Now he could write like a master.

"Now" correctly indicates a change in state, but it's a lazy substitute for stronger storytelling. That Babu couldn't write well before but *now* can is a foregone conclusion; otherwise, he wouldn't have blown one of his three wishes. "Now" doesn't tell us anything we couldn't have figured out on our own.

The genie granted Babu his first wish.

Babu closed his eyes, concentrated, poised his pen above a sheet of paper and began to write. After a few minutes, he smiled up at the genie standing cross-armed behind him. "I have always admired eloquent prose, but could never find my voice. Let's see those snobby New York agents turn *this one* down!"

"Then" is another common form of unnecessary filler.

Bernard climbed the stairs, then headed to his room.

Walter turned, then approached the tearful young lady.

Sequencing of events is not difficult to interpret, even if it isn't specified by "x happened, *then* y happened, *then* z happened." Events that occur *later* in the text are understood to happen *later*.

Bernard climbed the stairs and headed to his room.

Walter turned and approached the tearful young lady.

Clarifying that Bernard climbed the stairs before heading to his room or that Walter turned before approaching the young lady is stating the obvious. Readers will not assume these actions are simultaneous.

Some authors overwrite sequencing by *numbering* it.

First, I'll go to the store; then, I'll cook dinner.

First, I'll carve out a block of time; second, I'll find a solitary place; and third, I'll hammer out my novel.

Why create a numbered to-do list when a fat-free, gluten-free, sugar-free sentence is healthier for your prose?

I'll go to the store and cook dinner.

I'll carve out a block of time, find a solitary place, and hammer out my novel.

Though the first example logically implies I'll be cooking *at the store,* readers won't have difficulty interpreting my intention to bring groceries home to my own kitchen. If the logic bothers you, use "then" but don't number the actions.

I'll go to the store and then cook dinner.

Use your word processor's "find" function to search for instances of "then (usually preceded by a comma)," "first," "second," etc. Rewrite as needed to improve clarity, power, and tone.

TELEVISION LAND

As storytellers, teachers, and thought leaders, writers must cultivate a skill for communicating without blocking the spotlight, don't you think? Now tell me, isn't it annoying when you're watching a movie and one of the characters turns, faces the camera, and makes some remark to "the audience"—as if he's in a live show and you're sitting somewhere in "television land," ready to cheer or shout advice? I'm sure you'll agree that audience engagement must be managed cleverly. *The Rocky Horror Picture Show* pulled it off masterfully, but this style demon—a species of the editorial "we"—has the potential to ruin the relationship between the reader, the narrator, and the characters in a book—even if the narrator *is* the main character.

Talking directly to your reader is a bit like hugging a stranger. As warm and personal as that gesture may be, it will likely be perceived as an invasion of space. Your book is about what *you* think. Your reader doesn't owe you an opinion and even if she did, you *can't* be "sure she'll agree with you."

Asking anonymous readers for their opinions or support makes you sound insecure and in need of approval.

Having written a book, you have invited your reader to share your thoughts, ideas, feelings, memories, and experiences. Write boldly, humbly, and confidently. Stand behind your prose whether the reader likes it or not; some will and some won't. Ask your *editor* for a writing critique and then hand your *reader* your best shot.

Part of the "bargain" between writer and reader is that you, the author, get to share openly and intimately; the reader gets to consume your prose anonymously and without comment. A book is, in some respects, a "hidden camera" into your life and mind. "I see you peeking," hints from the writer make that relationship creepy.

If your goal is to make your writing sound conversational and informal, talking to the reader is no more effective than preceding sentences with crutches like "So," "Anyway," or "Also." Informal writing is direct and simple. Hints of humor, personal style, and uncomplicated language are all that's required.

If you're a graduate student, "we" is a status you hope will be conferred upon you after you graduate. Until then, you're subordinate to your professors; many will find your use of the editorial "we" inappropriate.

Talking to the reader (as I am now doing to you) is perfectly acceptable; that's what narrators do. I discussed the importance of the narrator's voice previously. But if I had written, *"We* discussed ..." in the previous sentence, I would have placed *you* in a conversation you hadn't consciously agreed to participate in. As subtle as that is, some readers find it manipulative or disempowering. *We never discussed anything.*

As with most style patterns in this book, exceptions abound. For example, it's appropriate to represent the voice of a committee or company by stating what "we" think.

Blind application of rules is no more effective than writing without thinking. Be conscious of the relationship between you and your reader. Establish respectful ground rules and stick to them. Consider each case individually, but unless you're the Pope or have parasites, the editorial "we" is best used cautiously.

CONCLUSION

If you keep writing, your work five years from now will be better than your work today. And your work ten years from now will be better than your work five years from now. Practice, improve, grow, and enjoy the journey. Accept that wherever you are on your steep climb up the literary mountain will be somewhere between base camp and a summit you'll never attain—and that where you are is an honorable place to be.

Too many writers work in isolation because they think they're "not good enough" to share their work—a tragic mistake. Seek the counsel of those farther up the trail; they were all once where you are now.

A few final tips:

- Keep writing, even if you think your work stinks.
- Join a local or online critique group. You'll meet writers of every level, and if your work really does stink, they'll help you figure out *why*.
- Use software tools like AutoCrit.com to find and expose many of the writing patterns described in this book.

- Pay attention to your word processor's spelling and grammar checker.

- No authority says your book must be written in any particular order. If you're having trouble writing the beginning, write the ending. Or start with your favorite sections and then connect the dots.

- Read everything you can; pay attention to other writers' styles.

- When you're done with your manuscript, put it away for at least a month. Come back to it with fresh eyes to see what you missed.

- Read everything you can about writing, publishing, and book design.

- When you're ready, work with a professional editor. Collaborating with an insightful editor is one of the greatest experiences you'll have as a writer.

- Don't use retail profits or popular acceptance of your book as a measure of your writing ability. Many brilliant books are poorly promoted, too esoteric, or too niche-focused for mainstream book buyers. Many so-called "bestsellers" fail to disclose they were at the top of the "Underwater Philosophy" subcategory of "Africa Studies" for three months straight. Some writers buy thousands of their own books and send them to the shredder because the contrived clout that comes with being a "bestselling" author lands them five-figure speaking deals. Good books aren't necessarily good *products*. Sometimes, dreadful books make excellent products. Don't confuse writing ability with publishing failure or success.

Becoming a powerful writer takes time and practice. Awareness is the most potent catalyst for growth and improvement. I hope the insights offered in this short book empower you to express yourself eloquently, deeply, and accurately in your own authentic voice.

ABOUT THE AUTHOR

Dave Bricker, MFA taught graphic design at an Arts University for thirteen years. His graphic design work won an Adobe Site-of-the-Day Award and his Flash flipbook technology was a semifinalist in the Adobe Design Achievement Awards. He is the creator of the <PubML>™ eBook platform, which includes a web-based eBook format and a set of intuitive visual ePublishing tools for WordPress.

An adventure traveler, he began living aboard sailboats at the age of 18, spent several years cruising solo in the Bahamas, and crossed the Atlantic on a wooden yawl in 1991. On these voyages, he encountered the unusual people, places, and circumstances that color his stories.

His books include three novels, *The One-Hour Guide to Self-Publishing,* and *The Blue Monk,* an IPPY Award-winning memoir of his sailing voyages.

He works with writers and publishers to edit and design beautiful books containing remarkable stories.

Read his popular blog on writing, publishing, and book design at TheWorldsGreatestBook.com.

Learn more about the <PubML>™ eBook platform at PubML.com.

COLOPHON

This book was set in Adobe® Garamond Pro, a typeface designed by Robert Slimbach based loosely on the original designed by Claude Garamond in the 1540s. Though digital type designers have taken many liberties with Garamond's original design, the longer ascenders and descenders and slightly smaller counters add a friendly, romantic feel to the type without sacrificing legibility.

The title and cover text is ITC Franklin Gothic originally designed by Morris Fuller Benton in 1902, then updated and reissued as a digital typeface by International Typeface Corporation in 1980.

The cover design and typography were inspired by Blue Note Records album cover art created by Reid Miles in the 1950s and 1960s.

The author's name on the cover is set in Bodoni Poster Italic, offered in digital form by the Linotype Type Foundry.

This book was written, designed, typeset, and published by its author to meet or exceed the highest standards of the publishing industry. Please be kind enough to post an honest review of your reading experience in the online bookstore or readers' forum of your choice. Thank you!

www.ingramcontent.com/pod-product-compliance
Ingram Content Group UK Ltd.
Pitfield, Milton Keynes, MK11 3LW, UK
UKHW041412180426
11947UKWH00007B/82